PRICELESS PEARLS

(Beads of stringed verses)

Gitanjali Kapoor

First published in 2020 by

Becomeshakespeare.com

One Point Six Technologies Pvt Ltd.

119-123, 1st Floor, Building J2, B - Wing, WadalaTruck Terminal, Wadala East, Mumbai, Maharashtra, India, 400022.T:+91 8080226699

ISBN - 978-93-90040-91-9

DEDICATION

To the hands that never tire blessing
to the heartful of love that's ever forgiving
Priceless Pearls with love!

To My Mother

PRICELESS PEARLS

PRELUDE

How do you define a mother, I wonder?
by the number of kicks you've given her in her womb
and everytime she smiled,
or by the number of bites on her swollen nipples yet
she happily fed you and never cried.

How do you define a mother?
by the stretch marks that she proudly flaunts
or by all those sacrifices of her desires and wants.

Everytime I've tried to pen on my Mum
I've fallen short of words,
who's love so pure, deeper than any ocean
my ink just doesn't seem to thank her enough.

Priceless Pearls, a book adorned with precious words from my heart is my dedication to the Woman I love the most, my Beautiful Mother, Bina Kapoor.

A lady with a bellicose attitude who worked passionately for more than 30 yrs with a leading Airlines beside being a doting mother and a loving wife.

An inspiration to many, the sunshine of my life. Here's to my friend, my soul mate and my pride, my PRICELESS PEARLS.

'Thrones are for Kings.
so they say,
hence she created her own realm,
in Bombay.
Beauty the sun bows to
when she strolls by the bay,
a lady of virtues and finesse
the finest bouquet.'

CONTENTS

ETHEREAL REFLECTIONS- My Soulful Verses

SANGUINE DREAMS
(Ethereal Poem)

Flow
through me
sanguine dreams
Visions unseen
Like moonlight dancing
'tween the blithe starry seams.
Intoxicating like wine
arousing my passion to write
flow through me zephyr Divinity
awakening my creativity.

'She's the champagne at dusk night plunges into,
she's the muse blushing poetry on the pearl dew
she's the wildfire at the horizon of a new dawn,
she's a euphoric rhapsody the stars envy upon.'

POETRY DRAPED IN CASHMERE THREADS

In silken weaves of gold and red
Was she moonlight in daylight
Or poetry draped in cashmere thread.

Her sari flowed with seamless grace
Like a full moon glowed her pretty face

Her stilettos a pair of crimson rose
Was she moonlight in daylight
Or priceless pearls of a quaint prose.

A bun she donned with locks of curls
She sure was an envy of big town girls.

Her aura cascaded with warmth of spring
Was she moonlight in daylight
Or a fabric of ethereal love string.

My mother, a lady with artistic poise
Bequeathed my life with unbound joys.

She carries within the fire of a thousand suns,

An eclipse can only becloud her light for a while

But it can't stop her peerless shine!

MY RUEFUL APOLOGY

I blamed my mother for the longest
For putting me in a boarding,
Little did I know she was doing her best,
putting her own desires at rest.

A working Mum protecting her daughter
from unseen disasters
She must've cried seeing her empty nest,
But all I did was blame her for my loneliness.

I don't remember thanking her enough,
when most of my unspoken dreams were also met.

I wish I was more responsive to her efforts,
in not clipping my wings but making them strong,
Blaming our parents is so easy,
When its our own thoughts
playing the wrong tune all along.

I wish I could give back even one percent,
of life's countless horizons
she sacrificed for my quest.

All I can say in return today,
Yes I'm blessed yes I'm blessed
for I have a mother who's the best.

"How would the eaglet find her wings if her mother didn't push her off the cliff..."

SHE IS NO ORDINARY

She plays with fire and risks her peace
for she is no ordinary.

She treads on shards and dreams beyond her reach
for she is no ordinary.

She lives on edge and for thrills has an affinity
for she is no ordinary.

She is misunderstood often as fragile for her serenity
yet she is no ordinary.

She is a woman with wings carving her own identity.
Yes! She is a rarity.

"For the magic of your prayers to manifest
you need to first believe in yourself."

ASHEN LEAF

An ashen leaf by the quay
holding on to her ebbing glint
A misfit in the lei
But sure to leave an imprint.

That night the winds sang a lore
She danced to its flirtatious hints
Starlit florets washed ashore
The waves sure did leave an imprint.

The sky an azure bedeck
I an ashen leaf
My heart a soulful wreck
dances to drown its grief.

These verses to me make no sense
Like in my tea a dash of peppermint
An ashen leaf lone in a forest dense
Her ballads sure shall leave an imprint.

"Stretch marks are cosmic glitters; I flaunt them with pride 'cause only a Goddess can deliver a new life..."

HER KOHLED EYES

She smiles with her eyes
Like sparkling pearls
Dancing on sunlit skies.

Her alluring precious jewels
Swaying to and fro revealing
Her doleful hidden self.

But only to whom she wants to
Her ethereal orbs illuminate her story
For rest they are merely
Two kohled eyes drowned in potpourri.

"Mysterious from out just like the Ocean
but beautiful deep inside like an Ocean bed,
full of love, warmth and strength,
gifts rare and precious like corals
for those in her life."
- A Woman

WOMAN DECODED

Let me decode for you today what is a woman...
Yes what and not who...
since you've always treated her as a commodity
and not human…

Let me define you every part of hers
from the womb where you spent nine months
to the vagina you worship but treat as a curse.

Do you know why she bleeds every month?
No not the scientific reason, but spiritually
it's her way to let go of the hurt she faces and to
harbour no animosity.
That's why she is so forgiving...

She carries fire in her belly
but she's so damn silly,
ignoring her self-worth, she in you seeks love.

Eh, nothing wrong in that, right?
Isn't she born to love and serve?

But today she fights...
Fights to live her life
Now tell me isn't that right?

At every phase she needed to prove her sanctity
or why do you think would "MeToo" be the
movement
of this century??

It's sad even on social media if a woman raises her
voice
is called a Feminist and names that rip her off
ruthlessly with shame.

Let me decode you her power…
She's the one whom Lord Krishna bows to in
Bhagavad Gita.

She is the Shakti this Universe's immortal energy.
She is Mariam, She is Mary
She is the Goddess one day you'll marry.

She's the wildfire who confining to norms of the
society happily douses her desires.
Look into her eyes
You'll find depth of sincere devotion.
Look into her Soul
You'll find solace from your commotions.

Finally let me decode you her mood swings that you
shun off so coolly,
Why should they bother you if you love her so truly.

Her hormonal changes do cause a chaos
But doesn't she bear your tantrums as if you were
menopausal throughout the year.

A woman is not a commodity
She is the benevolent energy...
Resist this fact and soon you'll be at her feet
for today she has unfurled her wings of fire
and is no more afraid to slay the demons
who try to rip her off her sanctity…

And just like Poetry
she walks kissing the falling leaves
a subtle mischief in every stride
a touch of enchanting mystery.

HERO

A woman is much more
than shimmer and lace,
She's fire and storm
robed with grace.

A woman is much more
than negligee and size zero,
She's about labour pain, breast feeding
and many a times being her own Hero.

A woman is much more
than Durga, Lakshmi, and Sati
She's Chandi, Kali and Shiva's Shakti.

The woman in me is much more than you see,
She needs no mirror to define her beauty,
her aura reflects like a moonful saga
of her opulent divinity...

The day the woman in the mirror enchanted my mind,

I stopped seeking approval from anyone besides those eyes.

ETHEREAL REFLECTIONS

My Soulful Verses

TO LORD KRISHNA WITH LOVE

Oh most merciful Krishna
just like the seashell
humbly adorns the shore,
allowing its waters
to cleanse it's maligned core
I place myself at your lotus feet
pleading You to purge my forlorn Soul.

Oh benevolent King!
However far I may wander
in my quest to sail the highest waves
may I never flounder.

Let me never lose sight of your sacred sky
and may the view from the stormy seas
be of a tranquil wonder.

Oh! the preceptor of the universe
be the calm breeze in my life's endeavours.
enlighten my path with your consciousness
for I am the sand and you are my shore.

Bestow me with the light to realise this truth
just like the magic flowing
from your magnanimous flute.

SPEECHLESS

Speechless thou leaveth me
With diamond studded necklace of dew on trees.

Every morning shineth your jewels before my eyes
But all I do in my sorrows weep.

Speechless thou leaveth me with untold mysteries,
As you roll out a carpet bedecked with stars.

Yet every night I dust not my palms
nor joineth them in awe
But hold on to my agonies.

Speechless thou leaveth me
How naïve if my eyes miss to see
And my heart feels not
The love bestowed by thee…

ODE TO THE GODDESS OF DAWN,

"THE SUN"

Oh how you sing so mellifluous,
You little halcyon feathers,
I woke up to your sweet murmur
Didn't you know I was here to lull
in the quietude of nature…

And as I meandered through the lush green
the cherubic whispers of breeze enthralled me.
Losing my senses to the ethereal trance
I soaked in bliss beyond all times eternal
and the seraphic dance.

Lo! behold I see an army of cashmere
marching over the lake
A prelude it seems
for the arrival of the majestic Queen.

But as soon as the sky
flamed in bewitching coral hue,
the lake became a mirror blue.
And I stood there in awe
watching the mist disperse
giving way to the Sun.

Beautiful she was, in ways
the eyes couldn't see,
the Goddess of dawn in golden glory.
She modeled her aura
reflecting like fire in water.
And then off she went
without a backward glance
whilst I stood there lost
in this supernal dalliance.

MORNING SONG

A cup over floweth of golden corns
On green meadows and azure ponds
As unveils the tangerine queen of morns.

Serene music floods the dawn
Flute played by birds, a mystical song
As pearls of dew the emerald tiara adorn.

I watch transfixed nature's aesthetic bond
My heart surges with love and beyond
A spiritual symphony as a day is reborn.

THE GOLDEN SUNSET

Like a rosette leaf dancing
at the crest of a celestial bay
I've seen her gracefully fade away
Plunging into nothingness,
a Golden Sunset...

I hear a song so serene
a song of homecoming
by the feathered quills of day
as she twirls in Sufian shades,
the Golden Sunset...

And in a voice humbly mystic
She promised me to rise again
from the dust of bereaving stars
into a golden flame...

Oh! look how she blushes
behind the Cimmerian veil,
plunging into nothingness,
an Ambrosial Sunset.

A JOURNEY TO WHERE MY SOUL BELONGS

Grains of time washed ashore
Misunderstandings mattered no more
All I had craved all along
Was this journey where my soul belonged.

Silent woods echoing deep
Trails left unaware
Whilst the mind was asleep.
All this while I had walked the tracks wrong
But now I was on the journey
where my soul belonged.

Stations passed, as the train sped
Uncaged I, emotions foregone and dead.
A blissful rain drenched me wild
with it's sacred song

All I had craved was this journey
Where my soul belonged.

With a spindle she sits every night

to weave memories,

Those silken threads some knotted some wrinkled,

her precious accessories.

TWO SHADES LIGHTER(Ghazal Poem)

I colour my hair these days, two shades lighter,
my Love like your doting gaze, two shades lighter.

Moon seems blurry tonight, I wonder why,
is it mist or your ebbing daze, two shades lighter.

Look the stars have lost their shimmer,
like my smile's waning craze, two shades lighter.

December you've come too early this year,
my heart's still a frosted maze, two shades lighter.

'Geet' you've yearned too long for spring,
this could be a passing phase, two shades lighter.

MY MUM WORRIES A LOT

Seeing my hair turn grey
And no man in sight far away
She worries I'll rot
My Mum worries a lot

With age catching up
Her heart aches for her buttercup
She worries like a crackpot
My Mum worries a lot

I wish I could hide it all
But a Mum can see through the walls
How pious is her love and caring thoughts
My Mum worries a lot

AND SHE SMILES

She applies kajal
to match her dark circles
And she smiles...

Her puffed up eyes
with a dust of concealer she hides
And she smiles...

Cracked parched lips
longing for the elixir of true kiss
her pink lipstick beautifully
creates a happy vibe
And she smiles.

Beyond these masks
she hides embers of betrayals and lies
shrill cries
of her indelible marks
of unfounded love
And she smiles.

KISS HER LIKE…

Kiss her like a flower-lady weaves a gajra,
delicately interlocking the fragrance
along with the jasmine buds.

Kiss her like every petal
is a passionate unsung story,
when lips entwine a wildfire billows
into a forevermore rhapsody.

Kiss her beads of pearls
unstring them into rhythms of a poetry
like the first dew of spring
on the frosted petals.

Kiss her fierce yet candidly
interlocking every loose knot
like the Jasmine buds holding the petals
with a sensuous warmth.

LIPSTICK

Of all my accessories
my most favourite are my lipsticks;
especially the luscious pink
like cinnamon spice,
it's my weapon in disguise…

I've fought many battles
wearing it to mock hypocrite eyes
for a girl is no more seen as a soul
but shamelessly judged
by her accessories and clothes.

You may call me bold
'cause I don't wear dull shades
and my aura is vibrant
like the euphonic midnight waves.

'I let my thoughts wander like birds
unchained, uncaged
like the playful flow of my words.'

HAIKU POEM ON NATURE

With frills in her skirt
She dances stealing glances
The kite in my hand.

Oh I hear her sing
The mellifluous Koel
Balmy Summer's song.

Bees hum cheerfully
As she unveils her beauty
Welcome Spring's glory.

Come sing me a song
Rose beckons the Butterfly
Love blooms, Nature smiles.

Birds, Bees and Sunsets
Humanity, Kindness, Love
Make Earth supernal.

'My nomadic verses stopover
to silently caress
Souls unknown
Hearts forlorn...'

MY TREASURE TROVE

A vintage diary or my treasure trove
Seasons it's witnessed from winter to love.
Bound with every emotional saga
My poems are nothing but messages from above.

Sometimes silently Angels whisper me words
Sometimes it's the midnight breeze
Sometimes little passerine birds.
My poems are nothing but messages from above.

I know the day I'll bury them away
Along with me in some bucolic grave
You'll hear them sing carols and hymns
for Angels guide what I write
I'm merely a puppet made of clay.

And so my Diary shall be an art of love.
for my poems are nothing
but messages from above!

ABOUT THE AUTHOR

Gitanjali Kapoor, well known and much revered in writer's world by her pen name "Laughing_Soul" is an articulate lady in her forties from Mumbai, India.

After carving a fulfilling career in the hospitality industry her Poetic soul found solace in penning words.

Author and Publisher of four Anthologies, "Priceless Pearls" is her debut solo collection of poems. She's making waves globally in the literary world with her work adorning various international publications.

She's also invented a poetry form called the "MirrorAlphoppbet" which is extremely cherished by writers worldwide.

-

Links:
Insta ID: laughing_soul_poetry

Her Interviews
https://medium.com/@mirakee.justwords/rendezvous-20-abe66400f067

What it feels like for a girl
http://toi.in/bEXuGa/a21ai

Her Books:
Crimson Kisses, Ishq-e-Watan, Cashmere Diaries, Stotram and now Priceless Pearls.

In her words "Poetry is when my Soul breathes through my words, pain bleeds through my ink and I witness a rebirth of my thoughts."

ACKNOWLEDGEMENT

Her hazel eyes
mesmerizing
like gleaming pearl drops
in golden skies.

Her mischievous curly tresses
leaving a trail of fresh air
wherever she passes.

Her euphoric smile
weaving fairytales,
like wildflowers on mountain side.

Her luminous aura
shy, demure
adorning a diamante tiara.

My Goddess Divine, my Mother
a lady of finest virtues and finesse
a woman like no other.

I can't thank my Gods enough for giving me "The Best Mum in the World".
To my precious dad Raman Kapoor, Thank you for everything Papa.
My darling brother Dinesh, love you for being my relentless pillar through life's ups and downs.
My aunt Suman and uncle Pradeep I'm blessed to have your selfless presence in my life.

To my publisher BecomeShakespeare.com, thank you for giving shape to my debut book, especially Devanshi Doshi for her sincere support.
I am highly grateful to this sweet girl, Baishali Deb for her technical insights and design.
To my friend Suresh KC, thanks for your timely help with the cover and Biraj bhai for your initial assistance.

Thanks to my friends who made the journey of Priceless Pearls a memorable one.

A very special thanks to my dear friend Ken Shutt for helping me decide the name "Priceless Pearls."

I owe heartful gratitude to all those who've believed in my words and made me their Laughing_Soul.
Thank you!

'THANK YOU MA'